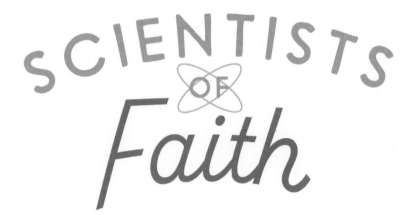

SUNBEAM

Published by Sunbeam, an imprint of Bushel & Peck Books.
All rights reserved. No part of this publication may be reproduced
without written permission from the publisher.

Bushel & Peck Books is a family-run publishing house based in Fresno, California, that
believes in uplifting children with the highest standards of art, music, literature, and ideas.
Find beautiful books for gifted young minds at www.bushelandpeckbooks.com.

Our family is dedicated to fighting illiteracy all over the world. For every book we sell, we
donate one to a child in need—book for book. To nominate a school or organization to
receive free books, please visit www.bushelandpeckbooks.com.

Type set in Tipique and Alkaline.
Illustrations by Wiliam Luong. Other graphic elements licensed from Shutterstock.com.

LCCN: 2023939910
ISBN: 978-1-63819-151-3

First Edition

1 3 5 7 9 10 8 6 4 2

SCIENTISTS OF Faith

28 STORIES
OF BRILLIANT
SCIENTISTS WITH
REMARKABLE
FAITH IN GOD

CHRISTY MONSON • ILLUSTRATED BY WILIAM LUONG

CONTENTS

1   GALILEO GALILEI 7

2   ROBERT BOYLE 9

3   SIR ISAAC NEWTON 11

4   MARIA MITCHELL 13

5   GREGOR MENDEL 15

6   GEORGE WASHINGTON CARVER 17

7   DOROTHY GARROD 19

8   HENRY EYRING 21

9   DAME KATHLEEN LONSDALE 23

10   GUADALUPE ORTIZ DE LANDÁZURI 25

11   KATHERINE JOHNSON 27

12   ABDUS SALAM 29

13   MEHDI GOLSHANI 31

14   FATHER BIENVENIDO F. NEBRES 33

15   DAME JOCELYN BELL BURNELL 35

16   GEORGIA MAE DUNSTON 37

17   PETER DODSON 39

18   AARON CIECHANOVER 41

19   WILLIAM D. PHILLIPS 43

20   MARY H. SCHWEITZER 45

21   FRANCIS S. COLLINS 47

22   DONNA STRICKLAND 49

23   ROSALIND PICARD 51

24   KATHARINE HAYHOE 53

25   JENNIFER WISEMAN 55

26   SUCHITRA SEBASTIAN 57

27   OMOLOLU FAGUNWA 59

28   KARIN ÖBERG 61

PUBLISHER'S NOTE

We're tremendously excited to present you with *Scientists of Faith*, a remarkable collection of true stories that perhaps couldn't come at a better time. Increasingly, it seems kids and adults alike find themselves presented with something of a false choice: to believe in God, or to believe in the work of science. We hope to offer a third choice: to let God inspire one's love of science, and to let science deepen one's wonder at God and His works.

In this book, you'll find remarkable men and women who did just that. These are scientists who were as devoted to faith as they were to their studies. Of course, the stories are as varied as the people themselves. Some individuals belonged to a specific religion or denomination. Others gravitated to a more general faith in God. Some changed faiths partway through life, some lost their faith and rediscovered it, and still others didn't discover faith until later on altogether. Some were Christian, others Jewish, and others Muslim. Their fields of study varied widely, from astronomy to paleontology to climate change. What they all had in common, however, was a sincere belief that faith and science go hand in hand.

We recognize that everyone who reads this book comes to its pages with their own personal beliefs about God and science, and that those beliefs will vary widely from reader to reader. For this reason, no one story in this book is meant to be seen as a standard or model of belief. Indeed, you might find that you disagree with the doctrine or theories of some of the scientists in these pages as much as you agree with others. That's okay! What we hope you will take from this book is not so much what to believe but how and why. From Galileo Galilei to Karin Öberg, we hope the examples of the men and women in this book will deepen your love of God and His wondrous creations and help you see how scientific curiosity can be a beautiful part of a faithful life. As it says in Psalm III:2, "Great are the works of the Lord, studied by all who delight in them."

> SOME STORIES COME WITH OPEN QUESTIONS. THERE ARE NO RIGHT OR WRONG ANSWERS. INSTEAD, THESE ARE MEANT TO HELP YOU THINK MORE DEEPLY ABOUT THE CONTENT. YOU MIGHT ENJOY DISCUSSING THEM WITH A PARENT OR FAITH LEADER, TOO. IT WILL BE A WONDERFUL CONVERSATION!

Galileo Galilei, an astronomer and mathematician, is considered one of the world's greatest scientists. Albert Einstein even called him "the father of . . . modern natural science," especially since he began the use of the scientific method of observations and calculations. He believed the sun, not the Earth, was the center of our universe.

Galileo was born February 15, 1564, in Pisa, Italy. His father wanted him to be a doctor, so he attended the University of Pisa to study medicine. But Galileo didn't like medicine. Mathematics was his favorite subject. His father wouldn't let him change from medicine to math, so he quit school altogether. He worked as a tutor and became so well known that the University of Pisa asked him to teach. In his public classes, he taught Aristotle's teachings, but in private, he and his students conducted experiments to see if Aristotle's ideas were really true.

At the time Galileo lived, the Catholic Church was very powerful and officially accepted Aristotle's philosophy on certain scientific subjects. Aristotle, though, wrote about his ideas as they made sense to him, rather than trying them out. Galileo believed that ideas needed to be tested to see if they were right.

For example, Aristotle wrote that heavier objects fell faster than light ones. Legends says that Galileo tested this by dropping objects like cannonballs, apples, rocks, and other things of different weights and sizes from the top of the Leaning Tower of Pisa. They reached the ground at the same time and proved Aristotle's idea was wrong.

Aristotle also believed that the Earth was the center of our solar system and didn't move. Nicolaus Copernicus, a scientist from Poland who lived before Galileo, suggested that the Earth circled the sun. Telescopes had just been invented in the Netherlands, so Galileo made one himself. But it was even better than the Dutch ones and magnified things twenty times bigger. Using it, Galileo was able to study Venus. Its shape changed during the year, so he knew that it revolved around the sun also. He concluded that Copernicus, not Aristotle, was right.

Galileo wrote about his discoveries in Italian rather than Latin, so more people could read them. The Catholic Church didn't agree with Galileo and called him to Rome to investigate him. Galileo argued, "I do not feel obliged to believe that the same God who has endowed us with senses, reason, and intellect has intended us to forego their use." Yet, in 1633 the church still convicted him of heresy (the crime of disagreeing with the church) and put him under house arrest for the rest of his life.

Four years later, Galileo went blind. Despite this and his punishment from the church, he never lost his faith. He died on January 8, 1642. In 1992, Pope John Paul II reversed Galileo's heresy conviction.

ASTRONOMER | MATHEMATICIAN

"God [is] the author of the universe, and the free establisher of the laws of motion."

Robert Boyle is called the "father of chemistry." He investigated nature through experiments and observation. He discovered the properties of gasses.

Robert was born on January 25, 1627, at Lismore Castle in Waterford County, Ireland, into one of the richest families in Britain. He was the 14th child and 7th son of Richard Boyle, the first Earl of Cork. His mother died in 1630 when he was three, so his sister Katherine, who was 15 years old, took care of him.

He began school at Eton College when he was only eight years old. He loved learning about chemistry, physics, earth science, and history. His teachers soon realized he was very smart. When he was 12, Robert traveled with his older brother Francis through Europe, along with their tutor. After returning to England, Katherine encouraged Robert to write texts explaining his Anglican—a form of Christianity—beliefs. Robert worried that scientists would forget about God. He believed the more scientists discovered, the more they should see God's handiwork and goodness. He said, "God would not have made the universe as it is unless He intended us to understand it." He also believed more people should be able to read the Bible, so he paid for it to be translated in into several languages, including Welsh and Arabic.

Robert eventually spent 12 years at Oxford University where he and his friends—including Christopher Wren, the famous architect, and John Locke, a noted English philosopher—created the Royal Society, an important place for experimental philosophy. When Robert left Oxford in 1668, he went to London to live with his sister Katherine, Viscountess Ranelagh. Katherine helped Robert set up a laboratory in her home, where he could continue his work.

Robert experimented with chemical compounds. He analyzed air to discover its properties, including how we breathe and how sound is transmitted through air. When he had an idea, he tested it with experiments and observations to see if his idea was true. For example, Robert built an air pump to study the mechanical properties of gasses. He learned that when a gas is pumped into an airtight container, it will shrink to fit into that space. But, even though it shrinks, pressure will build up in the container. This property of gas is now called Boyle's law.

He died just a week after his sister, on December 31, 1691, at age 64. They are buried side-by-side in St Martin-in-the-Fields, London. Robert left all his papers and research to London's Royal Society. His lectures on Christianity are still in use today. He believed God created the universe and hoped new discoveries would help everyone understand our world better.

CHEMIST

ROBERT BELIEVED THAT THE MORE PEOPLE DISCOVERED, THE MORE THEY SHOULD SEE GOD'S HANDIWORK. HAVE YOU LEARNED SOMETHING THAT HAS SHOWN YOU GOD'S HAND?

"In the absence of any other proof, the thumb alone would convince me of God's existence."

Sir Isaac Newton was a physicist and mathematician. He established the basic principles of modern physics, including his famous laws of motion. He was an important part of the Scientific Revolution during the 17th century. He was also a devout Christian and studied and wrote about the Bible. Many of his religious writings weren't published until after his death.

Isaac was born on January 4, 1643, in Lincolnshire, England. When he was 12, Isaac went to King's School in Grantham, where he lived at an apothecary (a shop that sells medicines). It is possible he first learned about the world of chemistry there. Nine years later, his stepfather died, and Isaac again went to live with his mother and, now, three little brothers and sisters. His mother pulled him out of school to become a farmer. He didn't enjoy farming, and instead of tending the cattle, he sat under an apple tree, reading. Legend says that an apple fell on his head and he thought of gravity, though he probably just *saw* the apple fall.

Isaac's uncle soon suggested that he go to Cambridge, where, besides his classes, he waited on tables and cleaned the rooms of rich classmates. Some of his science classes there included the works of Aristotle. Though Isaac learned the material, he wasn't very excited about it. Outside of class, he studied the new philosophers like Nicolaus Copernicus, Johannes Kepler, Robert Boyle, and René Descartes.

In 1665, the plague was everywhere, and Cambridge was shut down. Isaac went home and worked on his ideas on calculus, light and color, the telescope, laws of motion, and gravity. In 1667, he returned to school, received a master's degree, and became a professor of mathematics. In 1671, he showed his telescope to the Royal Society of London, and they made him a member.

Isaac believed that white light was a made up of waves and was a combination of all the colors. Another member of the Society, Robert Hooke, thought that light was made up of particles, not waves. (It turned out they were both right, as light has mass like a particle but behaves like energy in waves.) Hooke and Isaac argued, and Isaac became so emotional that he couldn't work anymore. He stayed at home from 1678 until 1684. During that time, Isaac organized his ideas into his book *Mathematical Principles of Natural Philosophy*, which is still one of the most important physics books today. In 1703, he became president of the Royal Society. He died March 31, 1727, at the age of 84. Isaac never lost his faith in God. He said, "All my discoveries have been made in answer to prayer."

 WHAT DO YOU THINK ISAAC MEANT IN THE QUOTE AT THE END? HOW MIGHT FAITH AND PRAYER PLAY A PART IN SCIENTIFIC INQUIRY?

"Every formula which expresses a law of nature is a hymn of praise to God."

Maria Mitchell was an astronomer and educator. She discovered a comet and was the United States' first professional female astronomer. She was raised as a Quaker, whose beliefs included equal education for both girls and boys.

Maria was born on August 1, 1818, in Nantucket, Massachusetts, to William and Lydia Mitchell. She was the third of ten children. Her father was an astronomer and taught her about astronomy, mathematics, surveying, and navigation. She also attended a local school. In the evenings on her roof-top balcony, she loved to peer through the telescope at the whaling ships off the coast, as well as the stars, planets, and even an eclipse of the sun. In 1836, she found a job as a librarian for the Nantucket Atheneum, but she kept her nights free to sweep the skies with her telescope.

During this time, her religious beliefs began to change. She called herself a religious seeker with a simpler faith. Though she no longer identified with a specific denomination, her faith in God remained strong.

On October 1, 1847, she saw a faint light in the sky through her telescope. It wasn't a star. Could it be a comet? Maria raced downstairs to get her father to come look. He thought it was a comet, too. They wrote a letter to Professor William Bond at Harvard, and he agreed. King Frederick VI of Denmark even gave her a gold medal for being the first to see the comet, which was soon named "Miss Mitchell's Comet."

Thanks to her discovery, Maria became known by other astronomers. The next year, she was elected to be a member of the American Academy of Arts and Sciences—the first woman to do so. In 1856, she traveled to Europe to meet fellow stargazers.

Maria eventually returned to Nantucket. The U.S. Civil War had just begun, so Maria helped with the antislavery movement and worked for women's suffrage (or the right to vote).

After the war, Vassar College asked Maria to come and teach there. They had a 12-inch telescope, the third largest in the United States. She loved taking her classes out at night to talk while they studied the stars and planets. She and her students published their findings in academic journals where only men had written before. Julia Ward Howe (abolitionist and suffragist who wrote the "Battle Hymn of the Republic") was one of her pupils. Maria also helped form the Association for the Advancement of Women and served as its president in 1873.

Maria continued to live true to the faith she described as simple, combining it with her scientific discoveries. She explained, "Scientific investigations, pushed on and on, will reveal new ways in which God works, and bring us deeper revelations of the wholly unknown." She died in 1889 at the age of 71.

ASTRONOMER

"Man must contribute his minimum work of toil, and God gives the growth. Truly, the seed, the talent, the grace of God is there, and man has simply to work."

Gregor Mendel is considered the "father of genetics." He was a *botanist* (a person who studies plants), teacher, and Catholic monk who explained *genetics* (traits we inherit from our parents) using math, now called *Mendelism*.

Gregor was born July 22, 1822, in Heinzendorf, Austria (now part of the Czech Republic). He began life on a farm with his family. As a child, he worked with his father, grafting fruit trees to get the best fruit. His father wanted him to labor on the farm, but Gregor's school teacher was impressed by his talent for learning and wanted him to continue his education.

Gregor went away to school in a town called Troppau, but his parents had a hard time giving him money for living expenses. He tutored other students to earn money to feed himself, but sometimes he still went hungry. Despite money troubles, he graduated in 1840 with the highest test scores in the entire school. His physics teacher, Friedrich Franz, recommended that he join the Augustinian Abby of St. Thomas in Brünn (now Brno, Czech Republic).

As a monk, some of Gregor's first duties were to visit the sick and the dying. Seeing people that way made Gregor depressed. He became so sad that he couldn't work, so the abbot had him try teaching. Gregor liked it, but he failed the teaching exam. So the abbot then sent him to the University of Vienna to learn about botany, zoology, chemistry, and physics.

When Gregor returned to the abbey from his studies, he began to teach and set up experiments. He grew almost 30,000 pea plants. He found that out of four plants, one received a *recessive gene* (a type of gene from one parent), two were *hybrids* (a mixture of different genes), and one received a *dominant gene* (another type of gene from one parent). He discovered that genes are given in pairs (one gene from each parent) and give the plant or animal its traits. In 1866, Gregor published his findings.

People didn't believe Gregor's findings at the time. He didn't try to promote his theory, and only a few copies of his research were available in libraries. Most of his papers were burned by the next abbot. Later, botanists and geneticists found the same results as Gregor, but not until about 1900. In Great Britain, William Bateson, a biologist, showed a new interest in Gregor's findings. Much more research and scientific evidence is available now, but in order to understand it all, students must still study Gregor's ideas. Today, his work is known as Mendel's Laws of Inheritance.

Gregor died in 1884, but his life as a monk and a researcher shows his love and dedication to his faith, and his love of science. He wrote, "The victory of Christ gained us the kingdom of grace and the kingdom of heaven."

BOTANIST | GENETICIST

GREGOR HAD TO WORK EXTREMELY HARD TO GET AN EDUCATION WHEN HE WAS YOUNG. HOW DO YOU THINK THAT TOUGH EXPERIENCE HELPED HIM LATER AS A RESEARCHER? IS IT POSSIBLE THAT GOD WAS PREPARING HIM? WHAT THINGS MIGHT HE BE PREPARING *YOU* TO DO?

"I love to think of nature as [a] broadcasting station, through which God speaks to us every hour, if we will only tune in."

GEORGE WASHINGTON CARVER

6

George Washington Carver was an agricultural scientist and inventor. He taught at Tuskegee Institute in Alabama and helped farmers grow peanuts and soybeans for food and made many other products from them.

George was born into slavery around 1864 in Missouri. He was born to an enslaved woman named Mary, who was owned by Moses Carver, a German immigrant farmer. George was no longer an enslaved child when slavery was abolished in 1865, but he stayed on the Carver farm (along with his brother, James) until he was about 11 years old. As George grew, he hungered for an education. Because he was Black, he wasn't allowed to go to the local school, but he did find a school he could attend about eight miles away. Over the next decade, he moved from town to town, putting himself through school.

Eventually, he was accepted to Simpson College, a Methodist college. George loved both art and nature and couldn't decide which to study. However, one of his professors, believing that no one would buy paintings from a Black artist, suggested he apply to the Iowa State Agricultural College (now Iowa State University). So, George gave up art and dove into the study of soils and plants, including crossbreeding to create stronger vegetation.

When George graduated, Booker T. Washington invited him to become head of the agricultural department at Tuskegee Institute, a college for Black Americans in Alabama. Many farmers back then thought that peanuts were just animal feed and tomatoes were poisonous. George invented over 300 uses for peanuts, including peanut oil, peanut milk, and even peanut paper—though not peanut butter as some rumors say. He became known as "The Peanut Man."

He also taught farmers about crop rotation. Many had raised cotton for so many years that the dirt had no more nutrients, so he had them grow peanuts and soybeans to improve the soil. The U.S. Department of Agriculture was impressed with his work and invited him to join their advisory board. George even gave President Franklin D. Roosevelt peanut oil to massage into his legs, hoping to cure Roosevelt's polio.

George also taught a Bible class at Tuskegee Institute on Sundays, and the class grew to three hundred students. George loved the Bible and was a man of great faith. He even described peanuts and sweet potatoes as "two of the greatest gifts God has given us."

George died on January 5, 1943. Henry Ford said of him, "Dr. Carver had the brain of a scientist and the heart of a saint." In 1990, he was inducted into the National Inventors Hall of Fame, one of the first Black Americans to receive this honor.

AGRICULTURIST

GEORGE WAS KNOWN FOR HIS LOVE OF PEOPLE. HOW DID THAT LOVE IMPACT HIS RESEARCH AND DISCOVERIES? HOW CAN A DESIRE TO SERVE OTHERS CHANGE THE WAY A SCIENTIST APPROACHES HIS OR HER WORK?

DOROTHY GARROD

Dorothy Annie Elizabeth Garrod was a pioneering archaeologist who discovered artifacts from the Paleolithic period. In 1939, she was chosen as the first female Disney Professor of Archaeology (no relation to Walt Disney) at Cambridge University.

Dorothy was born on May 5, 1892, in London, England, as one of four children. When she was a young adult, tragedy struck her family. Two of her brothers and her fiancée lost their lives in World War I (1914–1918) and a third one died of the Spanish flu in 1919. With so many deaths in her family, Dorothy felt she needed to do something special in life to help make up for their loss. During this time, she also converted to Catholicism. Her father, Sir Archibald Garrod, was head of the war hospitals in Malta, and because of Dorothy's interest in archaeology, he suggested that she explore the Stone Age ruins in Malta.

She already had a degree from Newnham College at Cambridge, but she loved searching the ruins so much that she went back to England to study archaeology at Oxford. After that, she took a job at the Institut de Paleontologié Humaine in Paris to study the cave art in the Somme and Dordogne valleys. She loved the on-site digs and excavations, and her excitement inspired her fellow workers. She explored more than 23 sites in Britain, France, Gibraltar, Bulgaria, Anatolia, Palestine, Iraq, and Lebanon. When unearthing remains in Mount Carmel's cave region in Israel, she found at least 10 *Homo sapiens* (humans) and two people with Neanderthal characteristics. One of the females was one of the most important fossils ever found.

As she explored the ancient sites and made new discoveries, Dorothy began to doubt her Catholic faith. While in Paris, though, she met Father Teilhard de Chardin, who became a lifelong friend and helped her renew her faith. As she brought her beliefs in line with her work, she developed an evolutionist belief of human origins blended with a belief in the Christian God.

In 1939, Dorothy became the first woman awarded the Disney Chair at Cambridge. Women didn't have the same standing as men at the university in those days, and Dorothy felt shy around the male professors. The men who had held the chair before Dorothy all had doctorates, but Dorothy couldn't even earn one because she was a woman. Cambridge chose her for the Disney Chair anyway, because she was the most qualified.

She retired from Cambridge in 1952 but continued to go on digs and excavate. As her health declined, she moved to a nursing home in Cambridge, the Sisters of the Holy Family in Bordeaux, where she died on December 18, 1968. She loved God and her faith so much that she wanted to die among her fellow believers. In fact, Dorothy's diaries reveal a strong religious conviction that stayed with her until her death. She is still known today as one of the most important archeologists in history.

ARCHAEOLOGIST

"Contemplating this awe-inspiring order extending from the almost infinitely small to the infinitely large, one is overwhelmed with its grandeur and with the limitless wisdom which conceived, created, and governs it all."

Henry Eyring was a top chemist and researcher and wrote more than 600 scientific papers and 10 books. He is best known for his theory of absolute reaction rates, which are one of the bases of modern chemistry. He was given the Berzelius Medal in gold, which is awarded every 10 years by the Swedish Society of Medicine for great contributions in chemistry.

Henry was born on February 20, 1901, in Colonia Juarez (now Chihuahua), Mexico, where his family belonged to the Church of Jesus Christ of Latter-day Saints. His father owned a large cattle ranch, and Henry learned to ride a horse almost as soon as he could walk.

In 1910, the Mexican revolution broke out, so Henry's family moved, eventually ending up in Pima, Arizona. The entire family worked to clear the land for their home and ranch. Henry settled into his new place and graduated from high school in 1919. He loved math and science and earned an engineering scholarship to the University of Arizona.

In 1923, Henry received a degree in mining engineering. After he witnessed a mining accident that killed several men, he went back to school to study *metallurgy* (the science of metals) and worked in a *smelter* (a factory that refines metal from the ore). But the smelter was dirty, smelly work. Discouraged, he went back to the University of Arizona as a chemistry teacher, and one of his professors suggested he attend the University of California at Berkeley for a PhD in chemistry. Henry liked that idea. He graduated in 1927 and worked several places before joining the chemistry faculty at Princeton University in 1931. He lived by his belief, "If you do a job well, the very best you can, the opportunities will open up."

Henry's main field of study was *chemical kinetics* (the speed or rate of chemical reactions). He had a great imagination and came up with good ideas for research. During World War II, Henry worked on classified projects involving explosives. Throughout his professional career, he received many scientific awards.

In 1946, the University of Utah asked Henry to be the dean of the graduate school and build the university into a major research center. The family decided to move to Utah where there were more members of the Church of Jesus Christ of Latter-day Saints. Henry loved people. While in Salt Lake City, he served in many positions for his church. Henry believed, "There isn't anything to worry about between science and religion, because the contradictions are just in your own mind. Of course they are there, but they are not in the Lord's mind, because He made the whole thing, so there is a way, if we are smart enough, to understand them." Henry became Distinguished Professor of Chemistry and Metallurgy at the University of Utah. The chemistry building there is named after him. He died December 26, 1981.

CHEMIST

HENRY BELIEVED "GOD MADE THE WHOLE THING." WHAT DOES THIS MEAN, AND HOW MIGHT THIS BELIEF CHANGE HOW A PERSON APPROACHES FAITH AND SCIENCE?

"If we knew all the answers there would be no point in carrying out scientific research. Because we do not, it is stimulating, exciting, challenging. So too is the Christian life, lived experimentally. If we knew all the answers, it would not be nearly such fun."

Dame Kathleen Lonsdale was a chemist and *crystallographer* (a person who studies crystals) who discovered new properties of crystals. In 1945, she was one of the first two woman to be admitted into the Royal Society of London.

Kathleen was born on January 28, 1903, in Kildare, Ireland. The youngest of 10 children, she loved to read and remember facts just like her father. Her parents separated when she was young, and her mother moved to Essex, northeast of London, with Kathleen and the other children.

Kathleen won a scholarship to Ilford County High School for Girls. She loved math and science, but she had to attend the boys' school, because her school did not teach these subjects. She won a scholarship to the Bedford College for Women, part of the University of London, when she was only 16 years old. Kathleen wanted to major in physics, but the headmistress told her she would never amount to anything in physics. Still, in 1922, she received the highest score in 10 years on her physics exams. In fact, one of her examiners, W. H. Bragg, asked her to join his research school at University College, London. She studied the structure of organic crystals and their X-ray patterns.

While she was at University College, she met Thomas Lonsdale, an engineering student. They married and moved to Leeds for Thomas's work. She then helped establish *crystallography* (the study of crystals) as a science. They also became Quakers during this time.

Over the next few years, Kathleen and Thomas had three children and moved back to London. Kathleen was so busy with her children that she couldn't find time to work in the lab, so W. H. Bragg found a grant for her to hire a nanny and come back to work—this time at the Royal Institution of Great Britain, where Kathleen earned doctorates for excellent research contributions. In 1949, she became a professor of chemistry and head of the crystallography department at University College, London.

As Quakers, Kathleen and Thomas didn't believe war was justifiable. During World War II, they hid refugees, and in 1943, Kathleen spent a month in jail because she wouldn't register for civil defense duties. She was shocked at the poor conditions she saw in the women's prison and worked for changes to the prison system after her release. She also joined the Atomic Scientists' Association, because she wanted to see all nuclear arms destroyed.

In 1956, Queen Elizabeth II gave Kathleen the title of Dame (Commander of the Order of the British Empire). Then, in 1966, a rare *meteoric diamond* (a diamond made from a meteor) was named lonsdaleite after Kathleen. She died in 1971, leaving a legacy as advocate for science, women, and her faith.

CHEMIST | CRYSTALLOGRAPHER

READ THE QUOTE ON THE LEFT. HOW MIGHT A FAITHFUL LIFE BE LIVED "EXPERIMENTALLY"? WHY MIGHT GOD WANT US TO WALK BY FAITH AND NOT BY SIGHT ONLY?

"I find God almost constantly in everything. . . . The certainty of having God with me on my path makes me eager to do everything, and I find it easy to do things I didn't like doing before."

Guadalupe Ortiz de Landázuri was a dedicated chemist and chemistry teacher. She was also the first female member of Opus Dei—a part of the Catholic Church—to be *beatified* (a step just below becoming a saint) by the Pope.

Guadalupe was born on December 12, 1916, in Madrid, Spain. Her father was in the military, and the family was assigned to Tetouan, North Africa. Scarlet fever damaged her heart—which bothered her the rest of her life. She slowly recovered, but her health remained delicate. She drew family and friends to her with her positive attitude and love of laughter. They described her as courageous and bold.

In 1932, the family moved back to Madrid, where Guadalupe graduated from high school. She decided to study chemistry at Universidad Central. There were only five women in the class. Her classmates said she was not only serious about her studies, but also friendly.

While Guadalupe was in school, the Spanish Civil War (1936-1939) broke out. Her father was arrested and sentenced to die by a firing squad. She stayed with her father all night before his death. She was shocked and upset, but after pouring out her heart to God, she forgave the men who killed him.

After the civil war ended, Guadalupe felt called by God to join Opus Dei, a Catholic organization that helped young men and women put God first while they continued their professional and daily lives. Along with her responsibilities with Opus Dei, she kept up with her university classes. In 1950, the founder of Opus Dei, Saint Josemaría asked her to open a mission in Mexico. She transferred to a doctoral program in chemical sciences in Mexico in order to do so. There, she encouraged university students to study hard and give service to the church. She went into the slums with a doctor friend to help the poor, and she helped open Montefalco, a retreat house and a school, from an old colonial hacienda. The college El Peñón also opened on this site.

Guadalupe eventually returned to Spain, where she continued to study and serve. She researched materials used to reduce heat loss through furnace walls and discovered that the ashes of rice husks were effective. The press commended her for the use of recycled materials in saving energy, and she won the Juan de la Cierva National Research Award in 1965. Then in 1968, at the University of Navarra, she set up the Center of Studies and Research of Domestic Sciences and taught chemistry. Guadalupe studied textiles as well, analyzing the fibers to see how they would wash and iron. The textile industry awarded her a medal for her research.

Guadalupe died on July 16, 1975. Her family, friends, and acquaintances remember her for her cheerfulness, her humility, and her courage. On May 18, 2019, Guadalupe was beatified. According to the Catholic Church, that means Guadalupe can bless those who pray in her name from heaven.

CHEMIST

"I'm just lucky—
the Lord likes me,
and I like him."

Katherine Johnson was a mathematician who did complex mathematics to help the U.S. space program. In May 1961, she calculated the information for Freedom 7, the United States' first human spaceflight, piloted by Alan Shepard.

Katherine was born on August 26, 1918, in White Sulphur Springs, West Virginia. As a little girl, she loved counting. She remembered, "I counted everything. I counted the steps to the road, the steps up to church, the number of dishes and silverware I washed . . . anything that could be counted, I did." Her teachers at school knew she was advanced for her age. She graduated from high school when she was just 13 and then started attending West Virginia State College. She studied math and French and graduated with honors when she was 18.

After graduation, Katherine took a public teaching position at a Black school in Virginia. In 1939, West Virginia University integrated their graduate schools, and Katherine was the first woman asked to attend. However, after one term, she left school to start a family with her husband, James Goble. When her children were older, she returned to school and teaching.

In 1952, Katherine took a job in the all-Black West Area Computing section of the National Advisory Committee for Aeronautics (NACA) in Virginia. Katherine and the other women computed the numbers for flight research and tests. In other words, they *were* the computers.

In 1957, the Russians launched their Sputnik satellite into space, sending Katherine's life rocketing in a different direction. She joined the newly formed space program when NACA became NASA in 1958, and she continued her math work in the West Area Computing section.

By 1962, there were mechanical computers that could help with the computations for the first manned flight around the Earth. But the astronaut, John Glenn, didn't trust the computers. He asked the engineers to get Katherine to run the same numbers as the machines. "If she says they're good, then I'm ready to go." The numbers matched, and Glenn's flight was a success. The United States was catching up with Russia in the space race.

Katherine also ran the calculations for the Apollo Lunar mission. She helped with the Space Shuttle and the Earth Resources Technology Satellite. Over her career, she also wrote or coauthored 26 research reports. She was the first woman in her division to receive credit as an author. Before that, the reports had no names on them.

Katherine was an active Presbyterian. She belonged to the Carver Memorial Presbyterian Church in Newport News, Virginia. She believed that it was the grace of God that let her do the things she did. Though Katherine experienced prejudice, she also broke down barriers.

President Barack Obama presented Katherine with the Presidential Medal of Freedom in 2015, the highest civilian honor in the United States. In 2016, NASA named a building after her—the Katherine G. Johnson Computational Research Facility. She died on February 24, 2020.

MATHEMATICIAN

"[A] sense of wonder leads most scientists to a Superior Being . . . the Lord of all Creation and Natural Law."

Abdus Salam was a theoretical physicist—someone who uses math, chemistry, and biology to understand the universe and how matter and energy work together. He won a scientific Nobel Prize in 1979 and was the first person from an Islamic country to do so.

Abdus was born on January 29, 1926, in Jhang, a small town in the Punjab province of Pakistan. His father was an educational official in the Department of Education. He was raised as a devout Ahmadi Muslim. Abdus had a lot of talent in mathematics and science—a talent his father nurtured by giving him time to study. When he was 14, he passed the entrance exam for Punjab University with the highest marks ever recorded. He rode his bike home to tell everyone about his test scores, and the whole village turned out to cheer for him. He loved math, but he was also skilled in Urdu (the national language of Pakistan) and English literature.

After he graduated from school, his father wanted him to work for the government. So, Abdus did as his father suggested and applied for the Indian Railways. But, because he had to wear glasses, he couldn't pass the eye exam. He also failed the mechanical test. Besides, at age 18, he was too young for the job. Abdus didn't mind. He went to graduate school and got a degree in math instead. In 1946, Abdus received a scholarship in mathematics and physics from Cambridge University in England. There, he earned a PhD and several awards for his writing and research, including the Smith's Prize for his contribution to physics at the school.

In 1951, Abdus went back to the university in Lahore, Pakistan, to teach physics. But, in 1953, riots broke out in Lahore, and Abdus faced persecution because of his religious beliefs. He belonged to the Ahmadiyya Muslims, who are not considered actual Muslims by many in Pakistan. Ahmadi Muslims were then banned from practicing their faith. Abdus decided to leave, and he returned to Cambridge to teach. Despite this, he loved his country and his faith. He returned to Pakistan in 1960 and served as the chief scientific adviser to the president from 1961 to 1974 and helped establish Pakistan's space program.

Abdus worked very hard at everything he did. His students loved him. When he finished a lecture, the audience would give him a standing ovation. He received lots of awards besides the Nobel Prize and gave all the money from the awards to poor developing countries for their physics students.

He also enjoyed the beauty of God's creations and spent his life searching for scientific truth, saying, "The Holy Qur'an [asks] us to reflect on . . . Allah's created laws of nature."

Abdus died on November 21, 1996. When his body was sent to Pakistan for burial, over 30,000 people attended the funeral to mourn his loss. The word "Muslim" has been removed from his headstone, but those close to him know he cherished his religion.

"Since man was made in the image of God (Genesis 1:26), . . . it was deemed possible that man could discern the . . . structure of the physical universe that God had made."

Mehdi Golshani is a physicist and philosopher who is a professor of physics at the Sharif University of Technology in Tehran, Iran. His fields of study include *particle physics* (the study of the smallest detectable particles) and *theology* (the study of religion). He is a member of the Iranian Science and Cultural Hall of Fame, and he has won many scientific awards.

In 1939, Mehdi was born in Isfahan, Iran (250 miles south of Tehran). As he grew up, he immersed himself in Islamic beliefs. Even though he studied quantum mechanics and physics, he also studied philosophy. He has written many papers and books on the relationship between science and religion, including the book *The Holy Qur'an and the Sciences of Nature*, which has been translated into several languages, including English.

Learning has always been important throughout Mehdi's life. He believes that a Muslim must always continue to learn. Mehdi studied physics at the University of Tehran and received his bachelor's degree there. He then came to the United States to study for his PhD at the University of California at Berkeley, which he received in 1969.

Mehdi believes that knowledge can't be separated into religious and nonreligious subjects. In Islam, there is unity in all parts of life. He writes, "The Qur'an refers to all existing things in the universe as the 'signs' of their Creator, and the system of the universe as the imprint of an omniscient designer and programmer. The study of the universe and what exists in it is considered as one of the most important means for the knowledge of God and the recognition of the majesty of its Creator." In other words, Mehdi believes that science helps explain God.

He also writes that science not only explains God, but also glorifies Him: "The cultural mandate, which appointed man to be God's steward over creation (Genesis 1:28), provided the motivation for studying nature and for applying that study towards practical ends, at the same time glorifying God for His wisdom and goodness." Mehdi loves both science and religion and continues to work to explain the connection.

MEHDI BELIEVES THAT SCIENCE CAN GLORIFY GOD. HOW MIGHT THIS BE? WHAT ARE SOME THINGS YOU'VE LEARNED ABOUT THE WORLD OR UNIVERSE AROUND YOU THAT DEEPENS YOUR LOVE OF GOD?

PARTICLE PHYSICIST

"We are grateful for the providence that created this universe. For believers, we would say this comes from the providence of God."

Bienvenido F. Nebres is a mathematician, Catholic Jesuit priest, and a humanitarian. He served as president of Ateneo de Manila University until his retirement in 2011 and helped direct other universities and businesses.

Bien was born in Baguio, Philippines, on March 15, 1940, during World War II. At times during the war, his family had to escape to the mountains. He remembers being carried on someone's back and having only black beans to eat, and he watched the airplanes dogfight overhead.

After the war, his family went back home to Bacnotan in La Union, Philippines, where his father practiced medicine. Bien attended the local elementary school. His teacher cared for the war prisoners that were still in the city, and Bien remembered throwing rice balls over the fence to the men. His sixth-grade teacher taught about the lives of the saints and priests, and Bien decided he wanted to become a priest.

He studied at Christ the King College, a Catholic school. Then, he went to Sacred Heart Novitiate in Novaliches to become a priest. Along with his lessons, he played a lot of basketball and read all the books in the library, including the comics.

In college, there wasn't a strong math program, so Bien read a college textbook by himself and completed all the problems in the book. Sometimes he asked for help, but he learned most of it by himself. He also studied about Greece and Rome as well as philosophy.

Bien attended Stanford University in California from 1965 to 1970 to complete a PhD in mathematics. He headed back to the Philippines in 1970 to teach and develop a math and science program there. Along with other scientists, he helped create a Southeast Asian Mathematical Society (SEAMS) in 1972 to support research and graduate programs.

Father Bien, as he lovingly became known, reached out to scientists in Australia and Japan to develop a network of schools that promoted science. From there he became involved in creating a good relationship for students with the business world. In 1990, as president of Xavier University in the Philippines, he brought together wealthy businesspeople to work with the poor to create more opportunities. He also played an active role in helping the Philippines change from a dictatorship to a democracy.

Father Bien led Ateneo de Manila University as its longest-serving president. He served in leadership positions in the Jesuit Order, and as of 2021, Father Bien celebrated 65 years as a Jesuit priest. Blending his love for science and mathematics with his faith has always been part of his life. He writes, "I find no real difficulties in faith and science as lived realities." Father Bien continues to work tirelessly for education, growth, and the good of his people.

MATHEMATICIAN

FATHER BIEN FOUND A WAY TO USE HIS PROFESSION TO HELP OTHERS, ESPECIALLY THE POOR. WHAT AREA OF SCIENCE ARE YOU INTERESTED IN? CAN YOU THINK OF WAYS IT COULD HELP OTHERS?

"The universe is very big—there's about 100,000 million galaxies in the universe . . . an awful lot of stars. And some of them, I'm pretty certain, will have planets where there was life, is life, or maybe will be life. I don't believe we're alone."

Jocelyn Bell Burnell is an astrophysicist—a person who studies celestial bodies, like planets and stars. She discovered radio pulsars in 1967 as a graduate student, but her professor, Antony Hewish, won the Nobel Prize for the research.

Jocelyn was born on July 15, 1943, in Belfast, Northern Ireland. Her parents were Quakers and raised her in their faith. Her father was an architect who helped with the Armagh Observatory & Planetarium, which was near their home. She loved to visit the staff and learn about the stars.

At school, Jocelyn wanted to take science classes, but that wasn't allowed. Girls were supposed to learn how to cook and cross-stitch. She said, "My parents hit the roof along with other parents and demanded a curriculum change." She studied hard but ended up failing a school exam to move on to higher education. That didn't stop her though. Her parents sent her to a Quaker school in York, England, where her physics teacher helped her figure out how to study and take tests. She went on to study at the University of Glasgow and did well. In 1968, she earned a PhD from the University of Cambridge. As part of her research, she built a radio telescope to study *quasars*, which are areas in space that send out large amounts of energy visible to radio telescopes.

In November 1967, while doing her research, she found a "bit of scruff" on the chart that tracked the stars. It was a signal that pulsed regularly. She and her professor didn't know what it was, so they named it "Little Green Man I" (LGM-I). It turned out to be a radio pulsar—a new discovery. Antony Hewish published their findings with both their names on it, but he received the Nobel Prize and she didn't. Many felt that was unfair, but she didn't let that discourage her. Jocelyn has since taught at various universities and has worked at several observatories, including one on Mauna Kea, Hawaii.

Jocelyn continues to be an active Quaker. She has served in leadership positions in her local church and the worldwide community. She tells people that her beliefs in religion and science "fit together very, very well." She explains, "In Quakerism, you're expected to develop your own understanding of God from your experience in the world . . . and it seems to me that's very like what goes on in 'the scientific method.'"

In 2007, Queen Elizabeth II knighted Jocelyn and gave her the title of "Dame." In 2018, Jocelyn was honored with the Special Breakthrough Prize in Fundamental Physics with a three-million-dollar gift for her fundamental contribution to the discovery of pulsars. She used the prize money to start the Bell Burnell Graduate Scholarship Fund to be used for female, minority, and refugee students to become physics researchers.

ASTROPHYSICIST

JOCELYN'S DISCOVERIES DIDN'T SHAKE HER FAITH. INSTEAD, SHE SAYS THEY HELPED HER DEVELOP HER UNDERSTANDING OF GOD. HOW MIGHT THIS BE?

"The science of the human genome beautifully reflects Biblical themes of human identity."

GEORGIA MAE DUNSTON

1944-

Georgia Mae Dunston is a professor of human genetics at Howard University. She is especially interested in how genetics influence our diversity and our immunity. She also founded the National Human Genome Center at Howard University.

Georgia was born August 4, 1944, in Norfolk, Virginia. Her father cooked at a barbecue wholesaler, and her mother worked at various jobs as a cleaner, dishwasher, and presser. Georgia attended the local Baptist church and sang in the choir.

Growing up, Georgia saw unfairness in the world around her. She was in grade school when segregated schools were made illegal. She lived in a society with tension between different races. But the Bible says that God created everyone to be equal. "How does that difference reflect His [God's] love?" These questions shaped her future research career.

In school, Georgia loved learning. She graduated in the top five of her high school and received a college scholarship to Norfolk State University in Virginia. There, Georgia majored in biology and studied hard. Once a teacher gave her a C on an assignment. She knew she had done good work and asked the teacher about it. He told her she was capable of more, so she studied even harder.

After graduating, Georgia tried to get a job in New York City, but no one would hire her as a scientist because she was Black. Still, she wanted to work in her field, so she went to graduate school at Tuskegee University and then the University of Michigan. After she graduated, she chose to do further research at Howard University in Washington, DC, where she also created a PhD program for medical microbiology research. At the time, many organ transplants for Black people failed because the test matches for cell data were from white people only—specifically those from Europeans. So Georgia researched genetic data from Blacks. Her research helped with conditions like asthma and cancer.

During the 1990s, Georgia worked with other scientists on the Human Genome Project. The study found that 99.9 percent of our genes are the same. "And yet each of us is unique," Georgia said. "We are literally part of one big human family. . . . Now the question is how we're going to reflect that knowledge in how we live."

Georgia has great faith in God and her Christian beliefs. She says of her genome research: "It affirms our belief in a human population that is incredibly diverse, yet undoubtedly one, created in God's image, redeemed by Jesus' blood, and united by the Holy Spirit in the renewing and reconciling work of the Church."

Georgia has received many awards, including the Howard University College of Medicine Outstanding Research award and the NAACP Science Achievement Award. Her work continues to have a big impact on how human genes are studied.

GEORGIA'S RESEARCH ON THE HUMAN GENOME STRENGTHENED HER BELIEF IN GOD'S LOVE FOR THE HUMAN FAMILY. HOW?

"We discuss our beliefs in the compatibility of science and faith because of the faith that we hold dear and cherish."

PETER DODSON

1946–

Peter Dodson is a *paleontologist* (a scientist who studies fossils) and has published many books and papers about dinosaurs. He is a world-leading expert on horned dinosaurs, and he currently teaches at the University of Pennsylvania School of Veterinary Medicine.

Peter was born on August 20, 1946, and grew up in South Bend, Indiana, in a Catholic household. He and his older brother, Steve, rode their bikes around the countryside finding fossils. He loved the film *Fantasia*, with its animated dinosaurs, and by the time he was 13, he decided he wanted to be a paleontologist. His father, a biology professor, gave him college books on paleontology to study.

After high school, he attended the University of Ottawa in Canada. When the curator of dinosaurs at the National Museum of Canada came to talk to the students, Peter connected with him for a summer job. Peter and his wife spent the summer at the Dinosaur Provincial Park in Alberta, sleeping in a tent and digging up bones. He was the first to write about *taphonomy* (the different ways dinosaurs were buried). He explained that some dinosaurs are buried whole, some bones are found near each other, and others are scattered in an area.

For his PhD, Peter studied the *Protoceratops* family tree at Yale University. He applied for a job at the University of Pennsylvania and was hired by the Veterinary School of Medicine. He wasn't a veterinarian, but he decided to "bloom where you're planted." He taught lots of courses there, including paleontology, veterinary anatomy, geology, history, philosophy, and religion.

Peter has taught thousands of students in his variety of classes, receiving numerous teaching awards. He once said, "My students have been so central to my life for the last 40 years." Many of his students have achieved greatness in their fields, and he has made several important discoveries himself. In 1986, he named and described *Avaceratops* (a small herbivore) and in 2004 a *Suuwassea* (a large dinosaur with a long neck). An ancient frog (*Nezpercius dodsoni*) was named after both him and the Nez Perce Tribe of indigenous people, located in the Pacific Northwest.

He and his students have traveled the world looking for fossils, to places like China, India, Madagascar, Egypt, Argentina, United States, and Canada. He loves all his dinosaurs—each in a different way, but his favorite one is the *Auroraceratops*, because it's named after his wife, Dawn. (*Aurora* means "dawn," the beginning of the day.)

Peter's faith has stayed strong throughout his career. He writes, "In a word, dinosaurs were the jewels of God's creation. By no means failures, they graced the planet for 160 million years. Like all of His creation, they gave Him praise. God loved dinosaurs."

HOW DID PETER'S UNDERSTANDING OF GOD'S LOVE INFLUENCE HOW HE FELT ABOUT DINOSAURS? HOW MIGHT ONE'S RELIGIOUS BELIEFS INFLUENCE THEIR SCIENTIFIC BELIEFS?

"To this very day, along with several physicians and scientist colleagues, I take regular periodical lessons taught by a rabbinical scholar on how the Jewish law views moral and ethical problems related to modern medicine and science."

Aaron Ciechanover is a biochemist. Along with two of his colleagues, Avram Hershko and Irwin Rose, he received a Nobel Prize in chemistry in 2004. He earned the prize for his research on recycling cell proteins, which work to keep our organs and tissues functioning. He discovered that a substance called *ubiquitin* breaks down old, unwanted cells.

Aaron was born on October 1, 1947, in Haifa, British Protectorate of Palestine, after his parents moved there from Poland. His mother was an English teacher, and his father a clerk in a law firm. His father's office was in the Arab section of the city, and Aaron describes that his mother stood on the balcony each day to watch for Aaron's father to come home safely. At that time, the fighting between the Jews and the Arabs made his travel dangerous.

Aaron grew up enjoying the beach, warm weather, and the beautiful Mediterranean Sea. But he also wanted to be a faithful Jewish citizen. He had an older brother serving in the military, and Aaron planned to follow in his footsteps. Aaron also studied Judaism and Zionism, along with his regular schoolwork.

Aaron loved biology and learning about the world around him. He collected flowers on Mount Carmel and pressed them to dry between the pages of an ancient Babylonian Talmud that belonged to his brother. His brother was angry because it ruined the sacred book. Aaron also collected turtles and lizards. He spent hours studying objects through a microscope that his brother brought back from England. He and his friends even tried to launch a self-propelled rocket.

Life began to change as he grew older. Aaron's mother died when he was 11, and his father died when he was 16. He went to live with his aunt and continue his education. He spent weekends with his brother and sister-in-law in Tel Aviv, Israel. "With the help of these wonderful family members, I managed to continue," he says.

Aaron studied biochemistry and graduated with an MD degree in 1972. Afterward, he served in the military, where he made lifelong friends and saw military action during the Six-Day War.

His research with Avram Hershko led to a PhD in 1981 and a Nobel Prize in 2004—and a wonderful friendship of over 30 years. As of 2023, Aaron is a distinguished research professor at the Technion–Israel Institute of Technology. He is a member of the Israel Academy of Sciences and Humanities and the Pontifical Academy of Sciences. He opened the Ciechanover Institute of Precision and Regenerative Medicine at the Chinese University of Hong Kong.

"In order to have an impact to leave the world differently than you entered, you need to take the unpaved road, and the unpaved road will take you somewhere you don't know. Something is waiting for you behind the corner that is unexpected."

BIOCHEMIST

"I believe in God. In fact, I believe in a personal God who acts in and interacts with the creation. . . . I believe in God because of a personal faith, a faith that is consistent with what I know about science."

William D. Phillips is a physicist who, along with scientists Steven Chu and Claude Cohen-Tannoudji, received the Nobel Prize in physics in 1997. Their work has led to the use of atoms in many practical ways today. He also is a Methodist and is proud of his faith. "Being an ordinary scientist and an ordinary Christian seems perfectly natural to me," he says.

William was born on November 5, 1948, in Wilkes-Barre, Pennsylvania, to William C. Phillips and Mary Catherine Savino. His father was Welsh and his mother Italian. Both of his parents were social workers and very supportive of his scientific curiosity.

From the time William was little, he wanted to know about the world he lived in. His parents bought him a microscope when he was about six years old. He mixed all kinds of things together, like milk and orange juice, and studied them. As he grew a little older, physics fascinated him. He didn't really know what a physicist did, but he wanted to be one, so he read lots of books about them. He set up a laboratory in the basement of his house where he could do his experiments. Sometimes he blew the fuses out and the electricity went off. Other times he burned things. But, his parents let him try new ideas.

When he was in the fifth grade, William was placed in a special "advanced" class. He studied advanced math and French. Learning French proved to be a good thing, because later in his career he could work with French scientists. He graduated from high school with honors and went on to study at Juniata College in Pennsylvania—where his parents and sister had also studied. He met his wife, Jane, in high school, and they married after graduating college in 1970. William and Jane then moved to Boston, where he went on to get his doctorate at the Massachusetts Institute of Technology (MIT) in 1976.

In 1978, William accepted a position at what is now known as the National Institute of Standards and Technology and began his work using laser light to trap atoms. This work led to his Nobel Prize. He and his colleagues discovered they could study the atoms better when they trapped them and slowed them down. Because of their research, atoms are now found in atomic fountain clocks and other devices and are used in the biochemical and biomedical fields.

William and Jane didn't attend church regularly when they were first married. But, in 1979, they joined the Fairhaven United Methodist Church in Gaithersburg, Maryland. William went on to help establish the International Society for Science and Religion.

In 1982, he received the Outstanding Young Scientist Award from the Maryland Academy of Sciences. William has received many awards in addition to the Nobel Prize, including being elected to the National Academy of Sciences and winning a Service to America Award. He is also a member of the Pontifical Academy of Sciences. Currently, he serves as a Distinguished University and College Park Professor at the University of Maryland.

"If you . . . let God be God, I don't think there's any contradiction at all between the Bible and what we see in nature."

Mary H. Schweitzer is a paleontologist who made an important discovery that changed the way scientists look at dinosaurs. She was the first to discover blood cells in fossils and, later, soft tissue in the bones of a *Tyrannosaurus rex.*

Mary Schweitzer was born in Montana, the youngest of three children, and was raised Catholic. Her interest in science began when she was five. Her older brother taught her to read before he left for college. He gave her a book titled *The Enormous Egg,* which tells the story of a boy and his huge egg that hatches into a dinosaur. She loved the book—and still does. While her brother was away, he sent her books from the Smithsonian because he wanted her to keep reading. When he came home to visit, she told him she would one day become a paleontologist.

In 1977, Mary received a college degree from Utah State University. Later, she returned to school, wanting to be a doctor, but with three small children, she thought that would be impossible. She considered teaching science, but then she sat in on a class about dinosaurs and was hooked. She later earned a PhD in biology in 1995 from Montana State University.

In 2000, a *Tyrannosaurus* skeleton was discovered in the Hell Creek Formation in Montana. Mary began studying the *femur* (thigh) bone. As she looked at the bone through a microscope, she thought she saw "round red structures only present in the [blood] vessel channels." She had found red blood cells in a dinosaur. After Mary found the red blood cells, she said, "I didn't publish for over a year. I was terrified. First of all, I don't like attention or the spotlight, and I knew this was going to get a lot of attention." People were doubtful when they first heard of her findings. For three hundred years, scientists thought that when an animal was buried, the insides rotted away. But, Mary found soft tissues in a 68-million-year-old dinosaur bone. Some scientists argued with Mary's findings, but more research proved that she was right. More soft tissue has been found in other dinosaurs—and even in a mosquito fossil.

She says that the more time that dinosaur bones sit out in the light and oxygen, the more the soft tissue goes away, making finds like hers rare and special. She hopes that others will continue this line of research even though it takes a lot of repetition with very special tools.

Mary's faith has continued even though some people tell her that the Bible and science don't go together. When she talks to students, she says, "To me it is so exciting to see God revealed through science."

Today, Mary works as the research curator at North Carolina State University. She currently focuses on molecular paleontology, which looks for DNA, proteins, and carbohydrates in ancient fossils.

MARY BELIEVES THAT GOD CAN BE PARTIALLY REVEALED THROUGH THE DISCOVERIES OF SCIENCE. IS THIS POSSIBLE? WHY OR WHY NOT?

"I believe God did intend, in giving us intelligence, to give us the opportunity to investigate and appreciate the wonders of His creation. He is not threatened by our scientific adventures."

FRANCIS S. COLLINS

1950–

Francis S. Collins is a physician who studies genes. He discovered the genes associated with *cystic fibrosis* (a genetic disorder that affects mostly the lungs) and *Huntington's disease* (a breakdown of nerve cells in the brain). He also served as head of the National Human Genome Research Institute.

Francis was born on April 14, 1950, in Staunton, Virginia. His father taught theater at a local college, and his mother wrote plays. The family wanted to live off the land, so they bought a farm and raised cows and chickens. Francis picked and shucked corn and milked the cows.

The family held musical parties at their home where Francis loved to play the guitar. The famous singer-songwriter Bob Dylan even came to visit. Francis didn't think he could sing very well, so he went to the local church to learn about choir music, even though their family wasn't religious. His mother told him the church's ideas didn't "make a lot of sense."

Francis was homeschooled until the sixth grade. Then he went to high school and graduated when he was just 16. Francis went on to college at the University of Virginia and then received a PhD in chemistry from Yale University. During his schooling, he decided he'd like to become a doctor. So, he earned his medical degree at the University of North Carolina at Chapel Hill. He loved his studies and did well, but he also enjoyed music and played in a band.

While he was a medical student, Francis took care of a patient who was dying of heart failure. She believed in God and was at peace with her coming death. Francis couldn't understand how she could be so calm. He felt that he would have been panicked. She asked him what he believed. He didn't know.

Francis began to search for God. He met with a pastor and read C. S. Lewis's writings about Christianity. His faith in God began to grow. He loved the beauty of nature and one day saw a frozen waterfall while hiking in the Northwest United States. To him, that was a sign God was with him, and he began believing that God and science could exist together. In 2006, he wrote a book titled *The Language of God*.

Francis directed the Human Genome Project, which discovered the genetic code of our DNA. He has also served as director of the National Institutes of Health (NIH) under three U.S. presidents—Barack Obama, from 2009; Donald Trump, from 2017; and Joe Biden in 2021. Francis retired from the NIH in December of 2021 to become President Biden's science adviser.

When President Bill Clinton honored Francis and his team of scientists in 2000, Francis said, "We have caught the first glimpse of our own instruction book, previously known only to God." Francis has written several books and has won many awards, including the Templeton Prize for his work in the fields of science and religion. Today, he continues to investigate many scientific and genetic projects.

"Almost every religion is about love."

Donna Strickland is an *optical physicist*—someone who studies how light works with matter. She received the Nobel Prize in physics in 2018 for *pulse amplification* (pulses of laser light), which is used in LASIK eye surgery and in cutting the glass for cell phones.

Donna was born on May 27, 1959, in Guelph, Ontario, Canada. Her mother was an English teacher, and her father was an electrical engineer. She attended McMaster University, because it had an engineering physics program where she could work with lasers. She describes herself as a "laser jock" because she loves playing with lasers so much.

She earned her PhD from the University of Rochester, The Institute of Optics in 1989. This is where she began the research of the laser techniques that led to the Nobel Prize. She said, "It is truly an amazing feeling when you know that you have built something that no one else ever has—and it actually works." Donna is only one of three female physicists who have won a Nobel Prize.

After her PhD, Donna joined the Princeton University technical staff and worked there until 1997. That is when the University of Waterloo in Ontario offered her a job as an assistant professor. When she received the Nobel Prize, the school hurried to make her a full professor. She said she was fine being an assistant professor, though. She loved her job working with lasers and that's all that mattered to her.

Donna is a member of the United Church of Canada, and her husband is a practicing Jew. They have met in the same church building for more than twenty years—Sundays for her United Church of Canada, and Saturdays for his Temple Shalom. Donna is the coordinator of the Sunday morning services and goes to the building early to make sure the bathrooms are clean and the hymnbooks are passed out. Attending church for Donna is about peace—finding peace inside herself. She enjoys sitting in the sanctuary and singing the hymns and thinking about the small part she plays in the world.

Donna also participated in the first international conference on what scientists think about religion. She enjoys life, science, and her faith. Currently, she is a professor at the University of Waterloo in Ontario, Canada.

OPTICAL PHYSICIST

> WHAT DOES DONNA LOVE ABOUT HER FAITH AND ABOUT ATTENDING CHURCH? HOW ABOUT YOU? IS THAT SOMETHING YOU CAN FIND IN SCIENCE ALONE? WHY OR WHY NOT?

"Digging into the models of how the emotions work, I find I feel even greater awe and appreciation for the way we are made, and therefore for the Maker that has brought this about."

Rosalind Picard is a computer and electrical engineer. She studies *affective computing* (the study of computers that record emotion and stress) in her media lab. She was elected to the National Academy of Engineering for her work with affective and wearable computing.

Rosalind was born in May 1962, in Boston, Massachusetts. She grew up in a happy home. "I was in a loving family," she said. "I had good friends. I did great in school."

Her family was not religious, and she didn't grow up going to church at all. Some friends would ask her to go to church, but she didn't want to go. She kept saying she had a stomachache until they quit asking. Then they asked if she had read the Bible. She hadn't. She agreed to read it and found "incredible wisdom in there. . . . What was in the Bible was based on a lot of solid historical events and a lot of incredibly wise and brilliant instruction."

Rosalind went on to get her bachelor's degree in electrical engineering from the Georgia Institute of Technology. Then, in 1991 she earned a PhD in electrical engineering and computer science at the Massachusetts Institute of Technology (MIT). Afterward, she joined the teaching staff at the MIT media lab and began to research how to give computers emotional skills. She explained, "The more I learned about it, the more I realized that . . . to really make machines smart, we needed to understand how emotion works in people." She and her coworkers use robots and wearable computers in their research.

Rosalind has become an active inventor and has developed wristbands that measure physical and emotional tension. Sometimes emotional signals come from deep inside the brain. This use of affective computing can help people with depression and post-traumatic stress. It measures feelings by recording eyebrow raises, smiles, frowns, a head tilt, and many other facial expressions. The devices Rosalind has invented help autistic children monitor their stress. The wristbands can also help people who have seizures by sending an alert before a seizure happens. These alerts have saved lives. Wristbands are also used in education to alert teachers when kids are bored. They can monitor sleep and dream patterns, count steps, and measure heart rate. They have so many valuable uses.

Rosalind is busy at work developing new technology, but she also uses her time to practice and explain her faith. "Sometimes colleagues ask, 'How can you believe that?' . . . I used to think the same—people who believed in any religion must have just not thought about it. . . . It's the opposite. I had not thought as deeply about it, and I think many of them have not thought as deeply about it."

COMPUTER/ELECTRICAL ENGINEER

READ ROSALIND'S LAST QUOTE. WHAT DO YOU THINK SHE MEANS BY THAT? IF A PERSON THINKS DEEPLY ABOUT GOD AND RELIGION, WHAT DO YOU THINK THEY'LL FIND?

"I grew up very much with the idea that the Bible is God's written word, and the universe is God's expressed word."

Katharine Hayhoe is an atmospheric scientist and she studies climate change. *Time* magazine listed her as one of the 100 most influential people in 2014.

Katharine was born on April 15, 1972, in Toronto, Ontario, Canada. Her father was a science teacher and a missionary. Her grandmother also had a degree in science education and loved teaching her eight children about science. Katharine grew up thinking that science was the most wonderful thing you could explore.

Every summer, Katharine and her two sisters learned to identify bird calls and flowers native to southern Ontario. One late night, her father took her to the park and showed her the Andromeda Galaxy through binoculars. She was amazed to see a different galaxy outside our own with just binoculars. Later, on a family vacation, they drove all the way from Canada to the Outer Banks of North Carolina to see Halley's Comet. The family owned a station wagon, so they could always carry a telescope with them. When Katharine was nine, her parents took the family to Cali, Colombia, where they served as Christian missionaries and taught science.

In college, Katharine studied physics and astronomy. She graduated from the University of Toronto in 1994. While in school, she took a class in atmospheric science and was hooked. She went on to study it for her master's degree, and later her doctorate, at the University of Illinois. She found that climate change was a global issue that affects our health, our food, and our water. Because of her faith and love for others, she decided to do everything she could to solve the problem of climate change and global warming that hurts the whole world.

In 1997, Katharine founded ATMOS Research. She became known for her ability to explain scientific reports in ways that everyday people can understand. She helps cities around the world decide how to conserve energy and use *clean energy* (electric, wind, and solar) to take care of the planet. She tells people not to waste food or other resources and asks them to protect and care for their neighborhoods.

The faith that began in childhood continues to play an important role in her life. She married a pastor, Andrew Farley, and often speaks about her belief that science and religion are very compatible. As she explains, "There's no miracle technology that will fix the problem for us. Our hope is ultimately placed in God.... We've been given things to take care of on God's behalf.... God has given us these tremendous gifts."

Katharine is very well known for her work. She has contributed to television documentaries and books about climate change. Today, she is a professor of political science at Texas Tech University and the chief scientist of the Nature Conservancy. She continues to lecture throughout the world on global warming and climate change.

ATMOSPHERIC SCIENTIST

"In Christian faith, our significance is basically given as a gift of love from God, who's responsible for the universe."

Jennifer Wiseman is a senior *astrophysicist* (an astronomer who studies the physical nature of the stars) at NASA's Goddard Space Flight Center. She discovered a comet that is partially named after her, 114P/Wiseman-Skiff.

Jennifer was raised in Mountain Home, Arkansas, on a farm where her family raised cattle. At night, she loved to walk with her parents and study the night sky. The trees, animals, meadows, and stars from one side of the Earth to the other inspired her. She grew up in a Christian family.

In the 1980s, she studied the famous author and astronomer Carl Sagan and his work. Her imagination soared when she saw moons revolving around other planets and close-ups of those planets. Her parents didn't get to go to college, but they encouraged Jennifer and her two older brothers to receive an education. She did well in school and was valedictorian at her high school.

After high school, Jennifer went to the Massachusetts Institute of Technology (MIT). While in school, she also served two internships—one at the Kennedy Space Center and the other at Lowell Observatory in Flagstaff, Arizona. In Flagstaff, Jennifer studied the night sky and discovered a comet, 114P/Wiseman-Skiff, which was named after her. She said this was an answer to her prayer, because she hadn't picked a subject for her senior paper. Now she could write her paper on the comet.

Jennifer earned her PhD in astronomy from Harvard University in 1995. When she first studied radio astronomy, she didn't think she would like it. But after she took a couple of classes, she found it fascinating. After she finished her doctorate, she continued her research at the National Radio Astronomy Observatory in Charlottesville, Virginia.

Jennifer loves giving talks at schools, churches, and community organizations. She says that people are fascinated with pictures of the universe, "They're awestruck by it just as I am." She also says, "Interestingly, I don't hear much about this conflict idea [between science and religion] in my daily work with scientists. When I talk to people, I find that most people really realize that there are deeper questions of life that science can't fully address, and they don't really see why there should be any conflict."

Jennifer is comfortable with both her religion and her science, and shares her ideas freely with everyone around her. Today, she acts as the senior scientist for the Hubble Space Telescope and makes sure the Hubble is working at its scientific best.

ASTROPHYSICIST

JENNIFER SAYS THERE ARE "DEEPER QUESTIONS OF LIFE THAT SCIENCE CAN'T FULLY ADDRESS." WHAT DO YOU THINK SOME OF THOSE QUESTIONS MIGHT BE? DOES YOUR FAITH HELP ANSWER THEM? HOW?

"I'm a Christian. I believe there is a purpose in life far beyond science."

SUCHITRA SEBASTIAN

26

Suchitra Sebastian is a physicist. She was named in the top 30 "Outstanding Young Scientists" by the World Economic Forum in 2013. Also, *The Financial Times* listed her as one of the top ten "Next Big Names in Physics."

Suchitra grew up loving hands-on science projects like building a rocket, handling a snake, or creating a circuit. She belonged to a family that traveled the world. She's lived in India, Great Britain, and the United States. Even though she has experienced different cultures and places, her favorite is India—the smells, the tastes, the sights, and the sounds.

A graduate of Women's Christian College in Chennai, India, Suchitra loved physics, but she also enjoyed other subjects as well. Acting and other extracurricular activities that had to do with the arts were especially fun for her. She received an MBA from the Indian Institute of Management in Ahmedabad and worked as a management consultant for a few years. But she missed the thrill of scientific discovery, so she went back to school and earned her PhD in physics from Stanford University.

After graduation, she received a research fellowship and then continued to do research and teach physics at Cambridge University, where she became a full professor of physics in 2020. "With physics, I'm passionate about it. It has the potential to revolutionize the world."

Suchitra has studied the organization of electrons in materials plunged into extremely low temperatures, put under lots of pressure, or exposed to intense magnetic fields. In these very different environments, the electrons connected to each other in surprising and unpredictable ways. Suchitra looks at many different materials to find the ones that act in unique ways.

She explained her approach to science by saying, "Who I am is at the heart of the science I do. . . . The person you are is integral to the science you do. . . . I choose to do extremely exploratory physics where I deliberately choose problems where I don't know what the answer is going to be. Other people . . . need to do the kind of physics where you have to be incredibly careful and take years setting something up."

In 2016, she became director of the Cavendish Arts Science program, which works to bring artists and scientists together. In 2022, Suchitra received the New Horizons in Physics Prize and the Schmidt Science Polymath award. Her excitement for research continues to shine through as she explains, "science is about exploring new worlds."

PHYSICIST

SUCHITRA IS PASSIONATE ABOUT PHYSICS, BUT SHE SAYS THERE IS "A PURPOSE IN LIFE FAR BEYOND SCIENCE." WHAT MIGHT THAT PURPOSE BE? HOW DOES YOUR FAITH HELP YOU FULFILL IT?

"Work and pray to live eternally in heaven with God."

OMOLOLU FAGUNWA

27

Omololu Fagunwa is a *microbiologist* (a scientist who studies microscopic organisms that cause viruses and bacterial infections). He has a PhD in theology and is finishing a PhD in microbiology at the University of Huddersfield, Yorkshire, England. He earned a Nigerian Presidential Honors award for his fight against AIDS, tuberculosis, and malaria.

Omololu grew up in the busy city of Lagos, Nigeria. (His name, *Omololu*, means "precious child.") His father worked for the government in the survey and real estate department. His mother was a small-scale businesswoman. Neither of his parents had any higher education, so they made sure their children went to the best schools possible.

The family's library was full of books and magazines about real estate and building materials. As a young man, Omololu came home after school and read about building and construction until he got bored. Then he'd get out his atlas to study and dream about people and landscapes in different countries around the world. He loved to draw, so his uncle—an architect—gave him drawing materials.

He grew up in a Christian home. He explains, "In my local church, I [led] about 10 other teens who were committed to knowing more about God. I was also involved in music, Bible study, and youth programs."

All through high school Omololu wanted to be an architect. He loved technical drawing and building design. But, deep inside, he had a passion for life sciences. After high school, Omololu followed his passion and studied microbiology at Olabisi Onabanjo University in Nigeria. He learned about *microbes* (tiny organisms only seen through a microscope) that caused disease and made people ill. He learned there were good microbes, too. "Some of these microbes bring variety, texture, and flavor to some of the food we eat all around the world," he says.

As he finished his degree, he worried that it would be hard to get a job in science. "However, God reassured me that all will be well, and that I am on the right track in my studies," he says. "After graduation, I held tight to the promises of God and using my microbiology training to improve rural health."

He began to use his knowledge in practical ways. Omololu helped the poor get access to medical care. He organized a mobile laboratory and medical outreach programs in areas that didn't have access to health care. He worked with the Federal Ministry of Health in Abuja, Nigeria, as scientific officer, creating policies and guidelines on food and medicine.

Omololu won a Nigerian national award and scholarship to study for his latest PhD and currently lives in England. He is also the host of a program on social media, "Called Scientist," which talks about science, Christianity, and development. Omololu continues to use his faith and science in whatever he works on.

MICROBIOLOGIST

"Wouldn't it be really cool to talk to another species that had a relationship with God?"

Karin Öberg is an *astrochemist* (one who researches chemical matter and living organisms on stars and in space). She is a professor of astronomy at Harvard University and studies star formation, planet formation, and the evolution of stars.

Karin was born on August 27, 1982, in Nyköping, Sweden. When she was six, the family moved to Karlskrona, where she grew up. As a young person, she was confirmed in the Church of Sweden, an evangelical Lutheran church, but her family did not regularly attend church. In high school, her chemistry teacher asked her to participate in an international chemistry competition. She won her local contest and was one of four students to represent Sweden at the international meet. Her father helped her with a research project that resulted in her first publication.

Karin came to the United States to attend the California Institute of Technology. "Caltech . . . taught me to think, to ask questions, and to solve problems as I scarce had thought my mind capable of," she says. She thought she could double-major in physics and chemistry, but then she discovered astrochemistry, a mixture of the two subjects.

Even though Karin belonged to the Swedish Lutheran church as a child, she found herself doubting her beliefs. While she was at Caltech, there were Christian students who kept God in her thoughts. She read C. S. Lewis's writings on Christianity and began to believe as he did. She also loved *The Lord of the Rings*, which she feels is "a remarkably Christian book."

To earn her PhD, Karin traveled to the Netherlands. While there, she researched *interstellar ice* (ice crystals and dust grains that make up the material that forms the solar system). She graduated with honors from Leiden University in 2009.

When she moved to Cambridge, Massachusetts, she converted to Catholicism. She said, "When I walked into a Catholic church and went to mass . . . it was an incredible sense of homecoming. . . . I think that was ultimately what cemented it." Karin is open about her faith with her fellow professors at Harvard and has had "many good discussions with my colleagues. I think it's important to have both kinds of stories out there—academia is often painted as a very dark environment for Christians, but it doesn't have to be."

Today, Karin is a full professor at Harvard University. She studies radio frequencies of young stars. She is interested in finding life on other planets, called *exoplanets*. As of 2022, scientists have discovered 4,034 exoplanets. Karin believes that 50 of those could be Earth-like. She wonders if there is life on them. "We do not yet know whether any of these extraterrestrial planets are inhabited or not, even by the simplest life-forms. Are we inhabiting a universe teaming with life . . .? Or are we a lonely ark, traveling through space and time carrying all living things with us?"

ASTROCHEMIST

FURTHER READING

Bardoe, Cheryl. 2015. *Gregor Mendel: The Friar Who Grew Peas*. New York: Abrams Books for Young Readers.

Becker, Helaine. 2018. *Counting on Katherine: How Katherine Johnson Saved Apollo 13*. New York: Henry Holt & Co.

Demuth, Patricia Brennan. 2015 *Who Was Galileo?* New York: Penguin Workshop.

Hollihan, Kerrie Logan. 2009. *Isaac Newton and Physics for Kids: His Life and Ideas with 21 Activities*. Chicago: Chicago Review Press.

Mills, Andrea. 2018. *100 Scientists Who Made History*. New York: DK Children.

Stabler, David. 2018. *Kid Scientists: True Tales of Childhood from Science Superstars*. Philadelphia: Quirk Books.

SELECT BIBLIOGRAPHY

"Aaron Ciechanover, Nobel Prize in Chemistry 2004: 'You Need to Take the Unpaved Road.'" YouTube, November 17, 2020. https://www.youtube.com/watch?v=LggDyclZxzk.

Beale, Stephen. "Why This Catholic Astronomer Is Hoping We Find Extraterrestrial Life." Aleteia, March 20, 2018. https://aleteia.org/2018/03/20/why-this-catholic-astronomer-is-hoping-we-find-extraterrestrial-life/.

Bosscher, Marcia. "The Unlikely Paleontologist: An Interview with Mary Schweitzer (Part I)." Women Scholars and Professionals, July 24, 2020. https://thewell.intervarsity.org/voices/unlikely-paleontologist-interview-mary-schweitzer-part-I.

Ciechanover, Aaron. "The Nobel Prize in Chemistry 2004." NobelPrize.org, n.d. https://www.nobelprize.org/prizes/chemistry/2004/ciechanover/biographical/.

Fagunwa, Omololu. Letter to Christy Monson, March 14, 2022.

Gianoulis, Tina. "Georgia Mae Dunston Biography," n.d. https://biography.jrank.org/pages/2401/Dunston-Georgia-Mae.html.

Gulshani, Mahdi. 2011. *The Holy Quran and the Sciences of Nature*. Selangor: Amin Research and Cultural centre(AARC).

Jackson, Ruth. "Professor Rosalind Picard: 'I Used to Think Religious People Had Thrown Their Brains out the Window.'" Premier Christianity, May 25, 2021. https://www.premierchristianity.com/interviews/professor-rosalind-picard-i-used-to-think-religious-people-had-thrown-their-brains-out-the-window/4359.article.

"Jocelyn Bell Burnell." Quakers in the World, n.d. https://www.quakersintheworld.org/quakers-in-action/366/Jocelyn-Bell-Burnell.

Khullar, Dhruv. "Faith, Science, and Francis Collins." *The New Yorker*, April 7, 2022. https://www.newyorker.com/news/persons-of-interest/faith-science-and-francis-collins.

McKee, Maggie. "An Explorer of Quantum Borderlands." *Quanta Magazine*, July 8, 2019. https://www.quantamagazine.org/suchitra-sebastians-quantum-explorations-20160609/.

Mitchell, Alanna. "How This Nobel Winner Balances Physics and Faith." Broadview Magazine, April 3, 2019. https://broadview.org/donna-strickland-is-a-church-lady-and-a-nobel-prize-winning-scientist/.

Moritz, B. M. "Peter Dodson." Science Meets Faith, n.d. https://sciencemeetsfaith.wordpress.com/tag/peter-dodson/.

Nebres, Ben, and Queena N. Lee. 2021. *At the Crossroads of Church and World.* Mandaluyong City, Philippines: Anvil Publishing, Inc.

Nobel Prize. "William D. Phillips, Nobel Prize in Physics 1997 – Interviewed in 2008." YouTube, November 22, 2019. https://www.youtube.com/watch?v=MFphKDuR0eE&t=39s.

Randall, Rebecca. "Georgia Dunston," February 17, 2020. https://www.christianitytoday.com/ct/2020/march/georgia-dunston-geneticist-christian-women-in-science.html.

Ruppel, Emily. "Not So Dry Bones: An Interview with Mary Schweitzer - Article." BioLogos, July 21, 2014. https://biologos.org/articles/not-so-dry-bones-an-interview-with-mary-schweitzer/.

"Scientists Speak about Religion and Science." Multifaith Education Australia, December 8, 2018. https://www.multifaitheducation.com.au/2018/12/08/scientists-speak-about-religion-and-science/.

Sequeira, Raquel. "Dr. Karin Öberg: Planetary Formation, Faith-Shaping Books, and the Beauty of an Intelligible Universe - Article." BioLogos, July 16, 2019. https://biologos.org/articles/dr-karin-oberg-planetary-formation-faith-shaping-books-and-the-beauty-of-an-intelligible-universe.

Tippett, Krista. "Katharine Hayhoe - 'Our Future Is Still in Our Hands.'" The On Being Project, May 3, 2023. https://onbeing.org/programs/katharine-hayhoe-our-future-is-still-in-our-hands/.

Unger Baillie, Katherine. "In Paleontology, Peter Dodson Is a King Begetting Kings." Penn Today, September 28, 2020. https://penntoday.upenn.edu/news/paleontology-king-begetting-kings-peter-dodson.

Valich, Lindsey. "Love at First Light." *Rochester Review*: University of Rochester, n.d. https://www.rochester.edu/pr/Review/V8INI/0501_nobel.html.

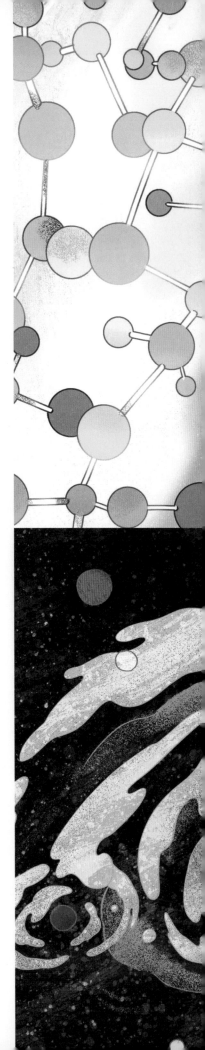

ABOUT THE AUTHOR

Christy Monson has a deep and abiding faith in God and has served in her faith community throughout her life. After retiring from a successful counseling practice in Las Vegas, Nevada, and Salt Lake City, Utah, she worked as an editor for the *Ensign* and *Liahona* magazines, religious periodicals for The Church of Jesus Christ of Latter-day Saints with a worldwide readership of over a million people. Christy earned a BA from Utah State University and an MS from University of Nevada at Las Vegas. She is a mother, grandmother, and great-grandmother, and loves working with children.

Her books include *Fifty Real Heroes for Boys*; *Love, Hugs, and Hope: When Scary Things Happen*; *Finding Peace in Times of Tragedy*; *Family Talk*; and the award-winning *Banished*. Connect with her at www.christymonson.com.

ABOUT THE ILLUSTRATOR

William Luong is an illustrator and graphic designer. He graduated from Dong Nai College of Decorative Arts as one of the top students in his class. His work is included in many books, including *The True West* and *50 Real Heroes for Boys*.

ABOUT SUNBEAM

Sunbeam is the faith-based imprint of Bushel & Peck Books. Sunbeam books are bridge-building: they work to create common ground between different faiths and between people of faith and the world at large. Our goal is to help kids and their families navigate an increasingly diverse and complex world with resilient faith in God and genuine love for all His children. Find more inspiring, faith-based books at bushelandpeckbooks.com.

ABOUT BUSHEL & PECK BOOKS

Bushel & Peck Books is a children's publishing house with a special mission. Through our Book-for-Book Promise™, we donate one book to kids in need for every book we sell. Our beautiful books are given to kids through schools, libraries, local neighborhoods, shelters, nonprofits, and also to many selfless organizations who are working hard to make a difference. So thank you for purchasing this book! Because of you, another book will find itself in the hands of a child who needs it most.

If you liked this book, please leave a review online at your favorite retailer. Honest reviews spread the word about Bushel & Peck—and help us make better books, too!

To nominate an organization or school to receive free books, simply complete the form at www.bushelandpeckbooks.com/pages/nominate-a-school-or-organization